EVALUATION PLAN FOR THE CAPE COD ADVANCED PUBLIC TRANSPORTATION SYSTEM

June 2000

PROJECT STAFF

Volpe National Transportation Systems Center
Robert Casey, Project Manager

Cambridge Systematics, Inc.
Christopher Porter, Principal Investigator
Tom Buffkin
Laurie Hussey

Acknowledgments

This report describes the evaluation plan for phases 1 and 2 of the Cape Cod Advanced Public Transit System (APTS) project. The Cape Cod APTS project is an application of Intelligent Transportation Systems (ITS) to fixed-route and paratransit operations in a rural transit setting. At the federal and state levels, the project is supported financially by the Joint Program Office for Intelligent Transportation Systems (JPO/ITS) of the Federal Highway Administration (FHWA) and the Federal Transit Administration (FTA) as well as the by the Massachusetts Executive Office of Transportation and Construction. The Cape Cod APTS project was initiated through a partnership between the Cape Cod Regional Transit Authority (CCRTA) and the Moakley Center for Technological Applications at Bridgewater State College. The project is supported locally by the Cape Cod Commission and the Cape Cod Economic Development Council.

The Volpe National Transportation Systems Center (Volpe Center) is responsible for the conduct of these evaluations for the FTA. The evaluation plan was developed by Cambridge Systematics, Inc. by Chris Porter, with assistance from Tom Buffkin and Laurie Hussey. The authors would like to thank Mr. Robert Casey of the Volpe Center for his assistance and guidance in developing the evaluation plan. The authors would also like to acknowledge Larry Harman at Bridgewater State College and Dennis Walsh, Bill Williamson, and Michael Gorss at the Cape Cod Regional Transit Authority for their assistance in identifying project activities and objectives, evaluation measures, and data sources.

Table of Contents

Table of Contents
(continued)

List of Tables

Executive Summary

The Cape Cod Regional Transit Authority (CCRTA) Advanced Public Transportation System (APTS) project is an application of Intelligent Transportation Systems (ITS) to fixed-route and paratransit operations in a rural transit setting. The purpose of the project is to apply ITS technology that will improve intermodal transportation services for the residents of rural Cape Cod as well as for visitors to the region.

The CCRTA fleet includes approximately 85 vehicles, and the service area covers 400 square miles. CCRTA's operations include an extensive dial-a-ride paratransit service, regional fixed routes, several community bus services, and seasonal village trolleys. While the paratransit system serves residents of the Cape only, the Cape is a heavy summer tourist destination, and the fixed-route services experience significant seasonal changes in demand. Peak summer traffic congestion can also significantly affect CCRTA's operations.

The Cape Cod APTS system is being implemented in a number of phases. Phase 1 took place over the course of 1998 and 1999, and Phase 2 is being implemented between January and May 2000. Together, these phases include:

- Installation of global positioning system (GPS)-based automatic vehicle location (AVL) technology on all vehicles in the CCRTA fleet;

- Deployment of Mobile Data Terminals (MDTs) on all vehicles in the CCRTA fleet, for onboard vehicle data collection and downloading of vehicle data and schedules;

- Installation of a multi-user base station using a GIS at the CCRTA dispatching/control center, to display real-time vehicle locations;

- Design and installation of a state-of-the-art fast local area network (LAN) for the scheduling system, and upgrading paratransit management software;

- Construction of a separate data radio system for data transmission; and

- A prototype Internet site that displays the location of vehicles in real-time.

A third phase, not considered in this evaluation, is expected to include the introduction of "Smart Card" electronic payment technology compatible with the MDTs deployed in Phase 2. Cooperative efforts are also underway with inter-regional carriers to develop an intermodal electronic payment system in the future. Implementation of these elements is anticipate to occur in 2001 and 2002.

The evaluation goals and measures developed for the Cape Cod APTS system are shown in Table ES-1. These measures reflect the overall goals and "few good measures" of the national ITS program. Corresponding measures have been identified for the Cape Cod

APTS project that reflect directly measurable benefits anticipated to both the transit agency and to local travelers.

Table ES-1 Evaluation Goals and Measures for Cape Cod APTS

Goal Area	National ITS "Few Good Measures"	Corresponding Evaluation Measures
Safety	• Reduction in crash rates	• Reduction in incident response time
Mobility	• Reduction in delay • Reduction in travel time variability • Improvement in customer satisfaction	• Average travel time or speed per trip • Advance time required to schedule trip • Schedule adherence • Provision of customer information • Customers/trips served • Customer satisfaction
Efficiency	• Increases in throughput or effective capacity	• Passenger trips per vehicle hour
Productivity	• Cost savings • Job satisfaction	• Staff time per task (calls, scheduling, maintenance, etc.) • Cost per passenger-trip or passenger-mile • Cost per vehicle-hour • Number of trips shifted to fixed-route transit • Staff acceptance

The evaluation will be conducted immediately following Phase 2 deployment, beginning in June 2000. To the extent possible, the evaluation will compare conditions prior to Phase 2 deployment with those following Phase 2 deployment, since most of the benefits will not be realized until after Phase 2 deployment is complete. The evaluation will rely heavily upon analysis of transit agency operational data, including historical data that have been archived. Customer survey data as well as financial data on system costs will also be utilized. Interviews with transit agency staff will be important in identifying impacts that cannot be quantified through other means.

The benefits of this evaluation are expected to extend beyond the knowledge gained by the Cape Cod Regional Transit Authority about the project's effectiveness. A significant objective of the Cape Cod APTS project sponsors is to demonstrate the viability of APTS technologies for rural transit operations. It is hoped that this evaluation will assist other rural transit operators throughout the country in assessing the full range of benefits and costs of APTS technologies, both to themselves and to their customers.

1.0 Introduction

The Cape Cod Regional Transit Authority Advanced Public Transportation System (Cape Cod APTS) project is an application of Intelligent Transportation Systems (ITS) to fixed-route and paratransit operations in a rural transit setting. The purpose of the project is to apply ITS technology that will improve intermodal transportation services for the residents of rural Cape Cod as well as for visitors to the region. The specific problems and issues to be addressed by the Cape Cod APTS project are:

- Access to jobs for year-round residents and the summer workforce;

- Integration of passenger transportation into an intermodal system by improved service design and effective and timely system information and payment mechanisms; and

- Severe traffic congestion in the summer tourist season on the region's highway system.

The success of the project will be measured through improvements in transit service, utilization, and customer satisfaction; and through improvements in operating efficiencies for the region's transit and intermodal passenger transportation services.

The Cape Cod APTS project was initiated through a partnership between the Cape Cod Regional Transit Authority (CCRTA) and the Moakley Center for Technological Applications at Bridgewater State College. The project is supported locally by the Cape Cod Commission and the Cape Cod Economic Development Council. At the state and federal levels, the project is supported financially by the Massachusetts Executive Office of Transportation and Construction and the Joint Program Office for Intelligent Transportation Systems (JPO/ITS) of the Federal Highway Administration (FHWA) and the Federal Transit Administration (FTA).

The project is an example of using the flexible funding provisions of the federal transportation statutes, and it is the first time federal ITS funds have been used for rural transit in a tourist economy. The project is built from a number of complementary efforts. The initial automatic vehicle location (AVL) portion of the APTS project and the evolution of a full-featured transit management center are a result of collaboration between the Cape Cod Commission and the CCRTA in response to a Congestion Management Air Quality (CMAQ) initiative. The GeoGraphics Laboratory at Bridgewater State College, financed by the FTA's Office of Research and Innovation, developed a geographic information system (GIS) route system for the Cape's regional intercity bus services as part of the FTA Transit GIS Database. FTA, through its Small Business Innovative Research (SBIR) program, funded the Viggen Corp. to develop a GIS Decision Support Environment, using the CCRTA as a prototype. A number of GIS analytical procedures have been employed to analyze paratransit and fixed route services for access to jobs (welfare to work) and recreational facilities.

2.0 System Overview

2.1 Transit System

CCRTA's intermodal transit operations are managed under contract to Ryder/ATE Transportation. Their operations include an extensive dial-a-ride paratransit service, regional fixed routes, several community bus services, and seasonal village trolleys. The CCRTA Local Area Network (LAN) is housed at the CCRTA operations center in South Dennis. There are approximately 85 vehicles in the CCRTA fleet, and the service area covers 400 square miles.

The Cape is a heavy tourist destination in the summer, and both demand and operation of the CCRTA system vary seasonally. The tourist season is considered to begin on Memorial Day and end on Labor Day. Demand on the fixed-route system, particularly the local trolleys, varies considerably by day of week and time of year. The paratransit system exhibits somewhat less variation, since services are limited to residents of the Cape only. The CCRTA system is also affected by roadway congestion during peak tourist times, whereas roadway congestion is much less of a concern during the off-season.

2.2 APTS System Deployment

The Cape Cod APTS project is a deployment of an ITS system to improve the efficiency and effectiveness of the CCRTA's operations and to provide more and better travel information to passengers and the transit authority's staff. The system is being implemented in a number of phases. Phase 1 took place over the course of 1998 and 1999 and included:

- Design and installation of a state-of-the-art fast local area network (LAN) for the scheduling system in Spring 1998;

- Installation of global positioning system (GPS)-based automatic vehicle location (AVL) technology on 20 vehicles over the course of the summer of 1998. In 1998 and 1999, these units were deployed on fixed-route vehicles during the summer season and on paratransit vehicles at other times;

- Installation of a multi-user base station using a GIS at the CCRTA dispatching/control center, to display real-time vehicle locations; and

- Construction of a separate data radio system for data transmission in the Mid-Cape area, with deployment of all Phase 1 AVL units on the dedicated data radio frequency for the 1999 summer tourist season.

Phase 2 is being implemented starting in January 2000, with planned full implementation by May 2000. Phase 2 components include:

- Upgrading paratransit management software to Microsoft SQL on an NT Windows LAN server;

- Deployment of AVL on all vehicles in the CCRTA fleet;

- Deployment of Mobile Data Terminals (MDTs) on all vehicles in the CCRTA fleet, for onboard vehicle data collection and downloading of vehicle data and schedules;

- Extension of the dedicated data radio system throughout the Cape region; and

- A prototype Internet site that displays the location of vehicles in real-time.

This evaluation will focus on the ITS components deployed in Phase 1 and Phase 2 of the project. Funding is currently being sought to continue the ITS deployment into a third phase. The primary element of Phase 3 would be the introduction of "Smart Card" electronic payment technology compatible with the MDTs deployed in Phase 2. Smart Cards would permit market-based pricing and automated billing and would gather customer information to support improved service planning. Development and testing is currently planned for 2001, with full implementation by Summer 2002. Cooperative efforts are also underway with inter-regional carriers to develop an intermodal electronic payment system in the future.

Under a separate but parallel effort, Bridgewater State College has developed a GIS-based decision-support system to aid in scheduling welfare-to-work clients. This will be integrated with an Internet-based travel planner that will be developed during the year 2000. This tool will assist client agencies and individual customers in planning trips by displaying bus routes and schedules that can serve a desired trip origin/destination and time. The Cape Cod APTS infrastructure and Smart Card will also be used to coordinate human services transportation and public transportation in the region.

2.3 APTS System Functionality

The GPS-equipped vehicles receive positioning data from orbiting satellites permitting each vehicle to know its location, within an accuracy of 10 meters (33 feet). Each vehicle uses a GPS receiver that can track up to six satellites that provide positioning data. The AVL system is made up of subcomponents including an intelligent vehicle logic unit (IVLU) and a modified radio unit. Transmission of GPS data takes place on a dedicated radio channel. Voice communications are conducted on separate radio channels.

A radio system previously used by a local fire department was obtained and installed for coverage of the CCRTA service area. The dedicated radio system minimizes data transmission costs and allows transmission of vehicle location data every 10 seconds or less. Positioning data is displayed at the CCRTA operations center on each vehicle dispatcher's CAD/AVL console. CCRTA has six CAD/AVL-equipped consoles. All CAD/AVL workstations display a detailed street map and colored icons representing the vehicles. The icon moves to the new location each time positioning data are received from the vehicle.

Another feature of the Cape Cod APTS is the emergency alarm. When an emergency alarm from a CAD/AVL-equipped vehicle occurs, dispatchers are able to immediately view the vehicle location. Furthermore, the radio dispatcher can activate a covert listening microphone on the distressed vehicle. By listening to the activities on the vehicle, in combination with "real-time" position information, the dispatcher can swiftly deploy emergency response personnel or take other mitigating action.

The Mobile Data Terminals to be deployed during Phase 2 will be used to transit messages from dispatchers to drivers and vice-versa, and to store data collected on board the transit vehicle. The MDTs include internal GPS to provide location information; a PC Memory Card slot for mass data storage or collection; an LCD display; an internal Smart Card and Credit Card reader; and a covert microphone.

3.0 Evaluation Goals

For the evaluation of the Cape Cod APTS project, there are both national and local goals. National ITS evaluation guidelines specify a "few good measures" that can form a common basis for evaluating projects. At the local level, the managers of the CCRTA have identified additional goals for the project. The following sections describe these various goals.

3.1 National ITS Program Goals

The National ITS Program identifies five goal areas that ITS projects might address:

- **Safety**, measured through a reduction in crash rates;

- **Mobility**, measured through reduction in delay and travel time variability, as well as improvement in customer satisfaction;

- **Efficiency**, measured through increases in throughput or effective capacity, as well as congestion relief;

- **Productivity**, measured through cost savings; and

- **Energy and environment**, measured through reductions in emissions and energy consumption.

Project sponsors have identified four of these goal areas – safety, mobility, efficiency, and productivity – as directly relevant to the Cape Cod APTS project. Although the project may have some energy and environmental benefits, these goals are not specifically addressed in this evaluation.

The National ITS program also identifies a "few good measures" associated with each goal area. The purpose of these measures is to establish consistency and focus across evaluations of a wide range of ITS projects. Alternative or surrogate measures may also be defined based on the available data and expected benefits for a specific project. In the current evaluation, alternative measures are defined that relate to the National ITS "few good measures" but are also specifically relevant to transit operations.

Table 3.1 summarizes the National ITS Program goal areas, associated "few good measures," and alternative or surrogate measures proposed for the Cape Cod APTS system. Table 3.1 also includes hypotheses regarding the various benefits of the system.

Table 3.1 Cape Cod APTS Evaluation Measures and Hypotheses

Goal Area	National ITS "Few Good Measures"	Surrogate or Alternative Measures	Hypotheses
Safety	• Reduction in crash rates	• Reduction in incident response time	• Incident response time will decrease as the ability of CCRTA to locate its vehicles is improved
Mobility	• Reduction in delay • Reduction in travel time variability • Improvement in customer satisfaction	• Average travel time or speed per trip • Advance time required to schedule trip • Schedule adherence • Provision of customer information • Customers/trips served • Customer satisfaction	• Scheduling/routing efficiency will increase, thus: - Reducing trip times - Allowing trips to be scheduled with less advance notice - Decreasing the size of the pick-up window • More customers can be served (for a given cost) as a result of increased operating efficiencies • Customer satisfaction will improve as a result of improved performance and information
Efficiency	• Increases in throughput or effective capacity	• Passenger trips per vehicle hour	• Improved operating efficiencies will increase transit system throughput/capacity
Productivity	• Cost savings • Job satisfaction	• Staff time per task (calls, scheduling, maintenance, etc.) • Cost per passenger-trip or passenger-mile • Cost per vehicle-hour • Number of trips shifted to fixed-route transit • Staff acceptance	• Through more effective scheduling, dispatching, and fleet control, the overall staff time requirements and hence cost per unit of service provided will decrease • Because of better information, some trips or trip segments can be shifted to fixed-route transit, thus reducing system-wide costs • The APTS technologies will be viewed as beneficial by transit agency staff in assisting them with their jobs

3.1.1 Safety

The National ITS Program identifies improvements to safety as an important goal of ITS projects. In the paratransit context, safety improvements mean improvements in the response to emergency incidents on paratransit vehicles involving either passengers or drivers. When a paratransit vehicle is involved in an accident, ITS technologies such as AVL can help identify the exact location of the vehicle, and thus speed the required emergency services to that location.

Indirect safety benefits may also be expected from the high-frequency (10-second) refresh capabilities of the AVL. First, dispatchers are able to observe vehicle speeds and identify cases of reckless or unsafe vehicle operation by drivers. By notifying drivers of the situation or taking punitive action, the AVL may reduce unsafe driving. Second, the AVL data may assist in re-creating accidents, determining causes, and implementing countermeasures. These benefits could ultimately lead to a reduction in the frequency and/or severity of crashes.

3.1.2 Mobility

The National ITS Program outlines mobility goals in terms of travel time improvements and increased customer satisfaction. Travel time improvements include both the reduction in overall travel time for passengers as well as the reduction in the variability of travel times so that passengers can better predict how long a trip will take. In addition to time savings, the provision of better information to travelers regarding travel options, anticipated travel times, etc. can also be considered a mobility benefit.

The National goals are directly relevant to the Cape Cod APTS project. Travel time benefits may include three components: (1) the average time it takes for a given trip; (2) travel time variability, as measured by on-time performance or schedule adherence; and (3) for paratransit, the advance time needed to schedule a transit trip. Reductions in travel time variability can also be measured through the size of the pick-up window required for paratransit trips. Qualitative or quantitative measurement of customer satisfaction can further describe the benefits of improved travel information and quality of service to transit customers.

An additional transit-relevant measure of mobility is transit system utilization. An increase in the number of passenger-trips suggests that people are provided with – and taking advantage of – greater mobility options. In the transit context, the recent welfare-to-work initiative has placed an emphasis on providing work-trip travel opportunities for low-income and/or mobility-limited clients.

3.1.3 Efficiency

The National ITS Program specifies that ITS projects should improve efficiency of transportation services. Efficiency is defined in terms of increasing throughput or effective capacity, as well as reducing congestion. Effective capacity is the maximum potential rate at which persons or vehicles may traverse a link or node under a representative composite of operating conditions. Throughput is defined as the number of persons or vehicles actually traversing a section of the transportation network per unit time.

In the CCRTA transit context, efficiency can be defined as maximizing the service provided per unit of transit operator resources. In other words, improvements in efficiency will be seen when the number of passengers served increases without a corresponding increase in resources used. Transit system efficiency is tied closely to productivity, and will be considered concurrently with productivity as discussed in Section 3.1.4.

In addition to improving transit system efficiency, the Cape Cod APTS may also have impacts on highway system efficiency, if customers can be diverted from personal vehicles to the transit system. This is viewed as a particularly important objective during the peak tourist season, when significant congestion is experienced in many locations on the Cape. The benefits to traffic congestion are a function of the number of people who shift from automobiles to transit. In this evaluation, impacts on vehicular travel will be the primary measure considered under "efficiency."

3.1.4 Productivity

The National ITS Program outlines two ways to calculate the costs savings of ITS. One is to calculate the difference in costs before and after installation of a system. The other is to compare the cost of ITS to traditional transportation improvements that are designed to address the same problem. To address the need for detailed data on costs of ITS, the evaluation guidelines contained in the Transportation Efficiency Act for the 21st Century (TEA-21) require that all projects receiving National ITS Program funds collect and report cost data on an annual basis. From these data, the productivity of the ITS project can be evaluated.

In the context of transit, total cost per passenger-trip or passenger-mile can be considered as an overall measure of transit agency productivity. This will be determined both by the *efficiency* of transit service provision (cost per vehicle-hour or vehicle-mile) and the *utilization* of the service (passenger-trips or passenger-miles per vehicle-hour or vehicle-mile). Overall efficiency, in turn, will be influenced by the monetary capital and operating costs of the ITS system and by changes in other staff time requirements, notably dispatcher, administrative, and maintenance staff time. Utilization will be influenced by increases in driver/vehicle productivity for paratransit and by increases in ridership for fixed-route service.

3.2 Cape Cod Regional Transit Authority Goals

Based on the Cape Cod APTS project documentation and discussions with staff, CCRTA has outlined seven main goals for implementing ITS technologies for their operations. These goals include:

- Improving dispatching operations;
- Reducing the cost per passenger trip;
- Showing that ITS can work for rural transit operations;
- Providing better passenger information;
- Promoting open, interoperable systems in ITS;
- Enhancing the amount and quality of the data available for planning and analysis; and
- Improving safety and security for transit operators and consumers.

These objectives are discussed below.

Improving dispatching operations. First, receiving and displaying accurate vehicle locations should enhance the operations of the CCRTA fleet. Dispatchers will have the ability to track a vehicle, compare its location to a prescribed route and time point, and advise an operator of late or early running on a route. On the basis of this information the operator can make necessary run adjustments. In addition to the field supervisors and the vehicle operators knowing that a vehicle is running off schedule, the dispatchers have the ability to see the extent of the problem and how it may impact other routes or blocks.

Reducing the cost per passenger trip. CCRTA hopes that the ITS technologies will reduce operating costs by moving passengers from paratransit service to fixed-route service, which is less expensive on a per-ride basis and can accommodate additional trips at little or no cost. The Authority has described this goal as achieving "greater efficiency and effectiveness through coordinated service delivery."

Showing that ITS can work for rural transit operations. A third objective is to show that ITS can work for rural transit operations, both operationally and financially. The unit cost per vehicle installation for the AVL equipment was approximately $17,000 in Phase 1 of the Cape Cod APTS project. Project sponsors believe that the unit cost should be closer to $4,000 in order to be affordable to rural transit operators. It is hoped that the Phase 2 implementation will reduce costs and will demonstrate the cost effectiveness of ITS for rural transit.

Providing better passenger information. This will be done through an on-line customer information system that would provide real-time location of vehicles, information about all types of transportation service including Steamship Authority ferry locations and schedules, and trip itinerary planning using off-the-shelf technology. CCRTA hopes to provide more consistent information that will promote ridership on their services.

Promoting open, interoperable systems in ITS. CCRTA believes that U.S. Department of Transportation will increasingly require that ITS implementations use open system architecture to encourage innovation and interoperability. CCRTA encountered difficulties in Phase 1 due to the closed systems that their vendors installed. For example, to compare scheduled versus real-time location of vehicles, the system would have required an interface between the scheduling software and the AVL software, created by the software vendor for an additional charge. CCRTA plans to deploy an open system architecture in Phase 2.

Enhancing the amount and quality of the data available for planning and analysis. The CCRTA sees the advantage of new data that ITS can provide, and considers the collection and analysis of these data one of the objectives of implementing ITS technologies. Currently, CCRTA believes that their existing scheduling and decision-making capabilities are fairly effective in addressing the immediate needs of an organization of their size. However, they would like to obtain more extensive data to gain a historical perspective on their operations. This will allow CCRTA to analyze their operations over time and to make strategic, long-term plans for transit on Cape Cod.

Improving safety and security for transit operators and consumers. Finally, CCRTA sees improved safety and security for transit operators and customers as one of the primary objectives of ITS in their operations. Their service area is rather large, and most of their vehicles do not operate on fixed routes. The ability of AVL to pinpoint the location of any vehicle in their fleet will provide them with an additional security feature that they believe will make their operations safer.

3.3 Relationship of CCRTA and National ITS Goals

The intent of the National ITS program goals is to measure the benefits of ITS technology to both the users and providers of transportation services. The hypothesis underlying these goals is that the ITS technology will allow transportation services to be provided with a higher level of quality and/or reduced costs.

The CCRTA goals for the Cape Cod APTS program are closely related to the National ITS program goals. In some cases, the CCRTA goals map directly into the national goals. Providing better information and service to customers corresponds to the national goal of improving mobility. Improving safety and security for transit operators and passengers corresponds to the national goal of improving the safety of transportation systems. CCRTA goals that focus on improving operations and reducing costs per passenger-trip translate directly into productivity improvements. These goals also correspond to mobility improvements, since lowering the unit cost of a trip allows more trips to be provided.

Other CCRTA goals should also lead to outcomes consistent with National ITS goals, albeit indirectly. Better data for service planning and analysis should help CCRTA adjust its services in the long term to become more efficient and to improve mobility for customers. CCRTA also hopes that by promoting open systems architecture and demonstrating the application of ITS technologies to rural transit systems, it can help other transit operators and customers throughout the nation recognize the benefits that may result from these new technologies.

4.0 Technical Approach

Section 4.1 discusses the general technical approach, including the technology impacts and expected benefits of the project; the time frame of the evaluation; and data sources available for project evaluation. Sections 4.2 through 4.6 discuss the various impacts expected from the APTS project, organized according to the National ITS goal areas of safety, mobility, efficiency, and productivity. These sections also discuss the proposed evaluation measures, data sources, and methodologies that will be used to assess the APTS project impacts.

4.1 General Approach

4.1.1 Technology Impacts and Expected Benefits

During the preparation of this evaluation plan, discussions were held with staff at CCRTA and Bridgewater State College to determine the operational impacts expected from the APTS system, benefits of the system, and data sources to support evaluation of these benefits. Table 4.1 lists the identified operational impacts, the associated ITS component(s), and the performance measures that should be affected. The hypothesis is that each ITS component has certain effects on CCRTA's operations, which then translate into "outcome" impacts or performance measures of safety, mobility, efficiency, and productivity. The ITS technology impacts are classified under the following headings:

- Real-time operational benefits;

- Data gathering and archiving benefits (for system planning and analysis);

- Direct staff time or staff productivity benefits and costs;

- Direct monetary costs; and

- Other benefits and costs.

Table 4.1 Cape Cod APTS Technology and Impacts

ITS Technology Impact	Technology — Phase 1/2							Phase 3[1]	
	AVL	GIS	Silent Alarm	10-sec Refresh	Upgrade hardware/ software	Internet/ cust info	MDT	Smart Card[2]	Trip planner
Real-time operational benefits									
Locate vehicles for incident response	X	X	X						
Improve schedule control	X	X							
Add last-minute requests	X	X							
Observe improper driver behavior	X	X		X					
Provide real-time info. to customers	X	X				X			
Implement more efficient pricing								X	
Data gathering/archiving benefits[3]									
Gather data on vehicle operations	X	X					X	X	
Gather data on customer trip patterns	X	X						X	
Reconstruct accidents	X	X		X					
Staff time -- benefits									
Speed dispatcher training/learning	X	X							
Reduce schedule program run time					X				
Eliminate need for paper schedules							X		
Reduce time communicating w/drivers							X		
Automate billing functions	X			X			X	X	
Staff time -- costs									
Time spent learning new technology				-- All --				-- All --	-- All --
Initial time investment				-- All --				-- All --	-- All --
Ongoing time requirements				-- All --				-- All --	-- All --
Monetary costs									
Equipment capital costs				-- All --				-- All --	
Maintenance contracts	X						X	X	
Replacement components				-- All --				-- All --	
Data transmission	X			X			X		
Other benefits/costs									
Provide system info. to customers	X	X				X			
Improve job satisfaction	X	X			X		X	X	X
Provide data to resolve complaints	X	X					X	X	X

Footnotes:
[1] Phase 3 elements will not be evaluated under this evaluation plan, but are shown here for cor
[2] Requires/works in conjunction with MDT
[3] Requires analysis of data and follow-up actions to result in benefits

Legend:
X = direct impact
(s) = secondary impact
+/- = potential positive or negative impact

Table 4.1 Cape Cod APTS Technology and Impacts (continued)

ITS Technology Impact	Safety — Incident response	Safety — Accidents	Mobility — In-vehicle time	Mobility — Reliability/ lateness/ delay	Mobility — Advance sched. time	Mobility — Cust. info	Mobility — Increase trips served	Mobility — Other cust. sat	Efficiency/Productivity — Driver/ vehicle	Efficiency/Productivity — Dispatch	Efficiency/Productivity — Admin.	Efficiency/Productivity — Maint.	Efficiency/Productivity — Direct costs	Efficiency/Productivity — Staff acceptance
Real-time operational benefits														
Locate vehicles for incident response	X													
Improve schedule control			?	X										
Add last-minute requests			+/-	+/-	X	X			X					
Observe improper driver behavior		(s)												
Provide real-time info. to customers						X	X	(s)						
Implement more efficient pricing								?	X					
Data gathering/archiving benefits														
Gather data on vehicle operations			(s)	(s)		(s)	(s)		(s)					
Gather data on customer trip patterns			+/-			(s)	(s)		(s)					
Reconstruct accidents		(s)												
Staff time -- benefits														
Speed dispatcher training/learning									(s)	X				
Reduce schedule program run time										X	X			
Eliminate need for paper schedules					X				X	X				
Reduce time communicating w/drivers									X	X				
Automate billing functions								?			X			
Staff time -- costs														
Time spent learning new technology									X	X	X	X		
Initial time investment														
Ongoing time requirements												X		
Monetary costs														
Equipment capital costs													X	
Maintenance contracts													X	
Replacement components													X	
Data transmission													X	
Other benefits/costs														
Provide system info. to customers						X	X							
Improve job satisfaction														+/-
Provide data to resolve complaints								X					?	X

Notes:
X = direct impact
(s) = secondary impact
+/- = potential positive or negative impact
[1]Requires analysis of data and follow-up actions to result in benefits

4.1.2 Timeframe

The current evaluation will focus on the combined Phase 1 and Phase 2 technologies that have been implemented beginning in 1998. Full deployment of Phase 2 is expected to be complete by May 2000. To the extent possible, the evaluation will compare conditions prior to Phase 2 deployment with those following Phase 2 deployment, since most of the benefits will not be realized until after Phase 2 deployment is complete.

Due to limitations in data and the phased nature of both system implementation and the resulting benefits, however, it is not possible to define a consistent and clear-cut "pre-implementation" and "post-implementation" time frame for all measures. Some benefits may have been experienced prior to full deployment of Phase 2, while others may take months or years to be fully realized. Furthermore, potential Phase 3 activities planned for 2001 may provide additional benefits in the future. As a result, an evaluation approach that can be extended to measure changes over a period of three to five years in the future is recommended.

Seasonality is another significant consideration in establishing the time frame of the evaluation. Because of the nature of the tourist economy on Cape Cod, there are significant seasonal variations in demand as well as environmental conditions (e.g., traffic congestion). Therefore, all information should be viewed in the context of the time of its collection, and quantitative changes in measures over time should be compared for the same season or adjusted to account for seasonal variations.

4.1.3 Data Sources

A number of general data sources are available to assist with this evaluation:

- Transit agency operating and financial records, including ridership, vehicle activity, farebox revenues, operating expenditures, and related data. These are archived on a monthly basis as well as submitted to FTA quarterly under standard reporting requirements;

- Transit agency incident reports;

- A call tracking system that monitors dispatcher call activity at the CCRTA operations center;

- Client databases maintained by CCRTA for paratransit customers, and by other local human service providers;

- Customer surveys of CCRTA paratransit and fixed-route customers, as well as a general survey of Cape Cod residents. These were previously conducted during 1998 and 1999, and similar surveys may again be conducted in the future;

- CCRTA financial records on items such as APTS capital and operating expenditures;

- Real-time vehicle activity data from the AVL system as well as passenger trip data (e.g., scheduled and actual pick-up and drop-off times) from the MDTs. Vehicle activity data are available for the Phase 1 period for the subset of vehicles on which

AVL was originally deployed. Vehicle activity and passenger trip data for the entire fleet, however, will only be available after full Phase 2 AVL and MDT deployment; and

- Knowledge of transit agency staff, including administrative staff, dispatchers, operators, and maintenance staff, that may be gained through interviews.

The following sections discuss the specific uses and limitations of each of these sources in more detail.

4.2 Safety

4.2.1 Incident Response

Impacts. "Incidents" requiring response can be classified into four categories: (1) accidents or crashes; (2) vehicle breakdown/maintenance; (3) passenger illness; and (4) disruptive passengers. According to transit agency officials, incidents of some sort on the CCRTA system typically occur about once per week. The AVL system combined with the "silent alarm" feature allows immediate location of a vehicle and appropriate response by dispatchers, who can then notify transit agency security, local law enforcement officers, or fire or medical services as necessary.

The most direct impact of the system should be a *reduction in average per-incident response time.* This is expected to result in some or all of the following "outcome" benefits to drivers, passengers, and the transit agency:

- An improved feeling of safety for drivers and passengers;

- Actual lives saved or injuries prevented or reduced; and

- Driver-hours and passenger-hours of delay reduced.

Data. The CCRTA keeps written reports on incidents. These include the time the incident occurred, but not the response time. Once Phase 2 is implemented, the MDTs will collect data that will indicate how long the vehicle was stopped, and therefore may allow the analysis of incident durations. Quantitative data, however, are not available for the "before ITS" case. Furthermore, such data would probably need to be collected over a relatively long time period, given the low frequency of incidents, in order to establish a statistically significant change in response time.

In the absence of quantitative data, dispatchers will be interviewed to identify changes in procedures for locating distressed vehicles, drivers and/or passengers, and will be asked to estimate the effect of the system on incident response time. Differences in response procedures by type of incident will be explored.

Other data will be required to translate the per-incident benefits into a more comprehensive estimate of benefits. These include:

- The frequency of incidents by type (obtainable from counting records), to translate benefits into annual terms;

- Driver-hours and passenger-hours of delay reduced (based on average passenger occupancy) and, potentially, the monetary value of these reductions (based on per-hour driver costs);

- Any benefits in terms of lives saved, injuries prevented or reduced, or perceived safety improvements. It is anticipated that these benefits will need to be evaluated qualitatively, through interviews with operators and other transit agency staff.

4.3 Mobility

Mobility improvements for customers may include any or all of the following components:

- Travel time savings for an average trip;

- Reduction in travel time variability or lateness;

- Reduction in advance time to schedule a paratransit trip;

- Availability of real-time and system information;

- Total number of trips served by the transit system; and

- Customer satisfaction resulting from improved service quality, information, etc.

These improvements will be measured as discussed below. The appropriate performance measures, as well as data availability, will differ somewhat between the fixed-route and paratransit services.

4.3.1 Travel Time Savings

Impacts. The combination of the AVL, GIS display terminal, and MDT data collection may result in travel time savings to passengers by increasing routing and scheduling efficiencies. In the case of fixed-route services, buses run according to a set schedule and therefore normal route travel times are not expected to change in the short run. The AVL/MDTs may provide long-term benefits, however, by providing data for planners to analyze system performance and make schedule adjustments accordingly.

In the case of paratransit services, the AVL system may allow greater scheduling and routing efficiencies to be achieved. On a day-to-day basis, the AVL/GPS display allows dispatchers to better observe real-time operating conditions and make any necessary scheduling or routing changes. In the longer term, the AVL/GPS can help dispatchers learn patterns more quickly and become more efficient in their scheduling and routing decisions. The overall benefits for an experienced dispatcher are likely to be small, but the system may help new dispatchers gain experience more quickly.

Data. Before deployment of the MDTs, the only available data from which to estimate trip times are schedules for fixed-route buses and for paratransit vehicles operating on semi-fixed routes. Aside from these schedules, data on point-to-point travel times at the trip or vehicle level are not maintained. Therefore, an initial assessment of this factor will be based on *interviews with agency staff* after Phase 2 deployment, to determine whether any schedule adjustments were made or are anticipated as a result of the AVL data.

The AVL data gathered during the Phase 1 deployment on 20 vehicles could potentially be used to gather baseline travel time data. Data on vehicle positions by time point could be used to observe travel speeds along various routes as well as dwell times at stops. Scheduled arrival times at specific time points could also be coded and compared to actual arrival times. Finally, trip data from a sample of time periods could be geocoded to observe trip lengths and travel times (Bridgewater State College has already geocoded trips for a week of Phase 1 data). Point A-to-point B travel times could then be compared before and after deployment of Phase 2, as well as at additional time points in the future.

Such an experiment would involve some effort to develop and analyze the data. It should be undertaken based on (1) interviews with staff to determine whether, and over what time frame, an improvement in travel times might be expected; (2) an estimation of the length of time and geographic scope for which data would need to be collected to demonstrate a statistically significant change, considering other factors that affect travel times; and (3) consideration of the feasibility of analyzing these data.

Discussion with agency staff should also indicate whether travel time improvements are anticipated to occur over time, following Phase 2 deployment. In this case, the AVL/MDT data can be used to compare travel times on various routes immediately following Phase 2 compared to a later point in time. If it appears that measurable improvements may be expected, a detailed data sampling and analysis plan should then be prepared for this factor. Note that if travel times are compared on a per-trip basis, rather than an origin-destination basis, trip lengths should be examined to ensure that they are similar in the "before" and "after" situations.

A final piece of information in valuing travel time improvements is the total travel time savings to riders. This requires additionally estimating the number of riders affected by travel time improvements. This may be estimated on a per-route basis or on a systemwide average (separately for paratransit and fixed route vehicles) from system operating records of passenger-miles and vehicle occupancy.

4.3.2 Travel Time Reliability/Lateness

Impacts. Travel time reliability is an important factor for travelers. In the context of transit, it involves comparing scheduled arrival/departure times of a vehicle (at a pick-up, drop-off, or time point) with actual arrival/departure times. More specifically, however, there is no single agreed-upon measure to describe reliability. The meaning and importance of this factor can vary depending upon personal needs, and there are also differences in definitions between fixed-route and paratransit travel.

For paratransit, discussions with agency staff indicated that scheduled vs. actual *arrival* time at the passenger's destination (away from home) is probably more important than scheduled vs. actual pick-up/drop-off time at home. In particular, many paratransit customers are going to appointments and do not want to be late for the appointment. More efficient routing and scheduling as a result of the AVL may help reduce the frequency of late drop-offs and/or the average lateness of drop-offs.

Another basic measure of paratransit schedule adherence is the size of the pick-up window that customers are given (e.g., customers are told that the paratransit vehicle will arrive at their house sometime between 2:00 and 3:00). With more precise scheduling procedures, schedulers may be able to reduce the size of this window.

For fixed-route service, reliability can be measured by comparing scheduled arrival times with actual arrival times at various time points along a route. Quantitative measures may include the percentage of time which a bus is late more than X minutes; the average difference between actual and scheduled arrival time; or the standard deviation of actual vs. scheduled arrival time.

Data. Prior to AVL deployment, data are not routinely maintained by the transit agency on actual vehicle arrival times, although the agency does conduct occasional schedule adherence checks for fixed routes. While agency staff indicated that dispatchers could potentially log arrival time information for a period of time for paratransit vehicles, staff were skeptical about the validity of the data and were reluctant to do this, given the many tasks that dispatchers must accomplish. Staff were also skeptical that logs maintained by drivers would contain accurate data on actual arrival times.

First, to get a sense of whether and how the APTS system may be improving on-time performance, interviews with dispatchers and other agency staff will be conducted to estimate:

- Whether there is any change in the size of the pick-up window given to paratransit passengers;

- The percentage of time paratransit trips arrive late, whether the APTS system may be helping to reduce this percentage, and why; and

- The percentage of time that fixed-route service gets "off-schedule," whether the APTS system may be helping to reduce this percentage, and why.

Second, for fixed-route services, data from recent schedule adherence checks will be reviewed to determine their adequacy for indicating schedule adherence improvements. In addition, the potential for using the Phase 1 AVL data to evaluate schedule reliability will be investigated. As with average travel time, this would involve geocoding paratransit trip origins and destinations for a sufficient length of time to observe any changes. It would also involve manually entering schedules and comparing scheduled to actual arrival times at appropriate points.

Also as for travel time impacts, the possibility of continued reliability improvements after Phase 2 implementation should be determined from discussions with agency staff. If such improvements are expected, a sampling and data analysis plan should be developed consistent with the plan for measuring travel time impacts.

4.3.3 Advance Time to Schedule a Trip

Impacts. The APTS may allow customers to schedule times more closely to the desired trip time. This may result from two factors. First, the MDTs will allow dispatchers to send the next day's schedules electronically to operators, rather than by fax as is currently done. Reservations currently are not taken after 11 AM of the day preceding the trip, due to the time required to prepare and distribute schedules. It is anticipated that the MDTs will reduce the advance time needed. Second, the AVL/MDT combination may allow dispatchers to insert same-day trips into schedules with greater ease. It is not anticipated that same-day trips will be normally be accepted, but they may be accommodated in exceptional circumstances.

Data. Items relevant to this factor will be obtained from interviews with transit agency administrative staff and dispatchers, and include:

- The latest time at which a paratransit customer can schedule a trip;

- Typical number of same-day trips accommodated; and

- Whether the APTS has allowed an increase in the number of same-day trips that can be accommodated.

4.3.4 Availability of Information

Impacts. The AVL system will make real-time information on vehicle locations and/or expected arrival times available to customers in the following ways:

- By calling CCRTA dispatchers (for paratransit trips);

- Via the Internet; and

- At video monitors that may be deployed, for example, in intermodal transit centers or shopping centers.

While all paratransit travelers will have access to this information via CCRTA operators, the benefit of other media outlets will depend on Internet connectivity as well as the number and location of video monitors. In addition to making real-time information available, the Cape Cod APTS may be able to increase the number of customer calls handled (including information requests) as a result of reducing the time required for other tasks. Currently, callers sometimes give up because the waiting time to talk to a dispatcher is too long.

Data. The availability and utilization of information will be tracked in the following ways:

- Analysis of call tracking system records to determine the number of customer calls processed, number of calls not completed, and the average length of time per call. Tracking system records are available for November 1999 and later (earlier records were inadvertently lost.) These records are kept in a format compatible with Windows programs including Microsoft applications, and should be archived for future analysis;

- "Hits" on the Internet web site;

- Interviews with agency staff to determine the number and locations of other outlets of real-time information;

- New questions for paratransit and fixed-route customer surveys regarding (1) availability of Internet; (2) utilization of real-time information from various sources; and (3) importance of real-time information to customers. These questions should be incorporated into customer surveys conducted in Summer 2000 and later.

4.3.5 System Utilization

Impacts. Another measure of mobility, in the transit context, is the total number of trips served. The hypothesis is that people benefit by having travel options available to them, and additional trip-making reflects additional benefits to travelers. The benefits of accommodating these additional trips will not be identified solely through a measurement of time savings or other benefits to existing riders.

For paratransit service, the number of trips that can be provided is essentially limited by two factors: (1) the agency's operating budget, which determines the number of vehicles and drivers available; and (2) the productivity of the agency as measured in trips per vehicle-hour. By making routing and scheduling more efficient, it may be possible to increase the number of trips accommodated by a single driver/vehicle over the course of the day, thus increasing the total number of trips that can be served for a fixed budget. In addition, cost savings in other aspects of the agency's operations, if large enough, could potentially allow resources to be shifted toward vehicle operation, thus increasing the number of vehicle-hours available.

In contrast to paratransit, additional ridership on fixed-route services has virtually no impact on operating costs as long as excess capacity exists. The APTS could potentially increase fixed-route ridership either by making service more attractive (e.g., through shorter travel or transfer times) or by providing more information about travel options to potential consumers. While some benefits may be realized immediately following Phase 2 deployment, CCRTA expects benefits to increase over time. Routes may be adjusted based on analysis of operating data, and additional information channels may assist people in planning trips.

The CCRTA also hopes to increase system utilization by shifting some paratransit trips to fixed-route service, thus freeing paratransit capacity for additional trips. This will primarily be a benefit of Phase 3, however. The mechanism for accomplishing these shifts will be to analyze travel patterns of paratransit riders (through MDT/Smart Card data) and target people who could potentially use fixed-route services instead, through information and fare incentives.

Data. Data on system utilization – both for paratransit and fixed-route – will be readily available for all phases of deployment. Monthly operating records are kept in hard-copy format that include the number of passenger-trips and passenger-miles by route. The data will be evaluated using *time-series analysis*. The analysis will consider whether increases in ridership occur following deployment of the various APTS elements, and whether these increases are statistically significant. The time-series analysis will account for seasonal fluctuations and will also consider other factors that might influence ridership, such as changes in the local economy or major events. Potential external factors will be identified through discussions with agency staff.

Because of the phased deployment of system components, lags in the adoption of resulting system improvements (e.g., schedule adjustments), and the response time for people to learn about and adopt to new services and information, it is not anticipated that an immediate jump in ridership will be seen following deployment of any particular technology. Rather, a more gradual increasing of ridership over time might be expected.

4.3.6 Customer Satisfaction

Impacts. Changes in customer satisfaction may reflect changes in the above mobility-related impacts, as well as any other improvements in convenience or quality of service that may result from the Cape Cod APTS. Measurement of customer satisfaction can help indicate both the perceived magnitude and the importance of each these improvements to customers.

Data. CCRTA conducted three customer surveys in Summer 1998: (1) a survey of paratransit riders; (2) a survey of fixed-route riders; and (3) a general survey of Cape residents. CCRTA plans to repeat these surveys in the future, with the next set potentially planned to start in Summer 2000. The surveys include a number of questions that measure satisfaction with CCRTA's services. The surveys should be reviewed to determine whether additional questions relevant to the Cape Cod APTS evaluation should be asked.

Another potential source of information on customer satisfaction is *customer feedback*, including comments, complaints, and praise. CCRTA only keeps records of written, not verbal, communication. CCRTA staff should be interviewed to determine:

- Whether they have received written correspondence (either complaints or praise) that they believe is related to APTS system functions, the amount of this correspondence, and the nature of the comments; and

- Whether they have received significant verbal feedback, either positive or negative, that could potentially be related to APTS system functions.

If a significant increase in written correspondence is noted, it may be worth examining these records to determine the nature and amount of the correspondence.

4.4 Efficiency

Impacts. For the purposes of this evaluation, "efficiency" is taken to mean roadway and traffic flow efficiency. Efficiency in transit operations is closely related to productivity and for the most part will be covered under productivity (Section 4.5). One specific measure, passenger trips per vehicle hour, could also be considered as an indication of transportation efficiency, since it describes the number of people moved per unit of service provided.

One of the goals of the Cape Cod APTS system is also to provide congestion relief, particular during the summer season, by accommodating trips via transit that otherwise would have been taken with a private vehicle. This coincides with the National ITS program goal of congestion relief. It is not anticipated that congestion relief benefits will be large enough to be measured directly, i.e. through measurement of traffic volumes and speeds. It may be possible to estimate the number of vehicle-trips or vehicle-miles of travel eliminated by the Cape Cod APTS system based on other data, including the total number of transit trips served by the system, the availability of automobiles to CCRTA riders, and the average trip length of a CCRTA rider. Even assuming that automobile availability data can be obtained, however, such an estimate would result in only a rough approximation of impacts on vehicle travel. Given that these impacts are likely to be relatively small, measurement of this factor is not recommended in the current evaluation.

Data. CCRTA keeps records of service provided, including passenger-trips, passenger-miles, vehicle-hours, and vehicle-miles, summarized on a monthly basis. Trends in passenger-trips per vehicle-hour can be analyzed over time using this dataset. This is the same set of data that will be used to assess ridership trends, and similar statistical methods will be applied to identify any significant trends and their relationship to implementation of the Cape Cod APTS system.

4.5 Productivity

Impacts. The Cape Cod APTS system is expected to influence transit agency productivity in a number of ways. These include:

- Direct costs of the system, including both capital and operating costs. Capital costs may include software, dispatch center hardware, in-vehicle hardware, and other hardware (e.g., radio transmission system). Monetary operating costs may include expenditures on maintenance contracts, parts and outside labor, and data transmission.

- Savings or increases in staff time spent on various tasks, as a result of the system. Some initial investment of staff time is required to become familiar with the technology, procure and install equipment, etc. This can be considered the equivalent of a capital expenditure in that it is a one-time, up-front cost. The Cape Cod APTS will also affect the time spent by staff on various repeated tasks. These include (but are not limited to):

- Dispatchers preparing and distributing schedules;
- Dispatchers answering calls and responding to customer requests;
- Dispatchers communicating with vehicle operators;
- Maintenance activities; and
- Training for new staff, for example, training time for new dispatchers to become familiar and efficient with scheduling and routing procedures.

- Increases in the number of passenger-trips that can be accommodated per vehicle-hour on the paratransit system.

- Increases in ridership on fixed routes, if productivity is measured in terms of passenger-trips served.

- Increases in farebox revenue may also be considered as a benefit to the transit agency that offsets additional operating costs.

Savings in staff time spent on various tasks may result in increased labor productivity for the transit agency. The value of these savings can be estimated by multiplying time savings by labor costs (including wage rates, benefits, and overhead) by position. These time savings, however, may not directly show up in the agency's "bottom line" since the agency tends to operate on a fixed budget. Instead, they may be reflected in other benefits; for example, the ability to accommodate more paratransit trips, or the ability of dispatchers to handle more customer information requests. As a result, productivity improvements are not reflected purely through measures of cost per trip provided.

An important measure that is related to productivity, but may not directly linked to it, is job satisfaction for transit agency staff. The APTS technology may make tasks easier or more difficult, therefore changing the level of effort or stress level involved. For example, the MDTs may make the vehicle operator's job easier by reducing the need to use the voice radio while driving. It may also provide other perceived benefits or impacts. For example, staff may feel more comfortable because they can more closely monitor driver behavior; on the other hand, drivers may view this as an intrusion on privacy. Anecdotal evidence demonstrates another benefit of the AVL to both drivers and other transit agency staff: the locations of vehicles can be verified, thus allowing customer complaints about missed pick-ups to be resolved (often in the driver's favor).

Data. Records of capital costs for all components of the APTS system as well as monetary costs for maintenance contracts will be available from transit agency records. Agency staff will be asked to track any significant additional expenditures on parts or outside labor related to the system. Staff will also be asked to estimate changes in other costs related to the system, such as data transmission costs.

For the most part, quantitative records will not be available to directly measure the staff time spent on various tasks. Instead, staff will be asked to estimate the various tasks on which they have spent more or less time as a result of the APTS system, and the approximate time increases or savings for each. Staff will also be asked to estimate whether they are able to accomplish more tasks (e.g., more contacts with customers) or to work more effectively as a result of the system. It is not expected that staff will know these amounts exactly or will be able to keep logs that track time spent by task. Instead, the qualitative answers will be used to identify the order of magnitude of savings on various tasks, and thus to identify which savings may be significant (and which may not) compared to other system costs and benefits.

It is anticipated that quantitative data will be available from the computerized call tracking system employed by CCRTA. This system tracks the number of calls handled by dispatcher station and time period, the length of time of calls, number of calls not handled, and other information. Calling patterns in particular could be affected by the MDTs, which will allow dispatchers and drivers to transmit messages electronically instead of by voice. A more detailed investigation should be conducted of the potential of these data to assess changes in call handling before and after APTS implementation, and a data analysis plan should be developed.

Data on job satisfaction and other non-quantifiable transit agency benefits will be gathered through interviews with transit agency staff. The questions will focus on issues such as:

- Whether the various APTS technologies and the additional information provided have been helpful in executing job duties, and why;

- Whether jobs have become easier or more difficult as a result of the APTS technologies, and why; and

- Staffs' overall impression of the project's impact on the transit agency's operations.

4.6 Other Issues

While not directly tied to the ITS program goals described above, additional issues should be considered in the evaluation that may have affected the success of this particular project. These include, but are not limited to, the following:

- Functionality of the APTS system, including reliability, accuracy, and ease of use;

- Agreements and relationships with equipment vendors;

- Institutional arrangements or considerations that may have led to particular successes or problems encountered; and

- Local environmental factors (e.g., geography, travel patterns) that may have led to unusual benefits or impacts of the system.

These factors will be assessed through discussions with the Cape Cod APTS project manager and CCRTA staff, and through continued quarterly reporting by the Cape Cod APTS project manager. These discussions and reports should provide a good source of information on the technical aspects of the project as well as unique local institutional factors.

5.0 Workplan and Responsibilities

The workplan is divided into the following primary tasks:

- Task 1 – Initial coordination;

- Task 2 – Revise and analyze CCRTA customer surveys;

- Task 3 – Conduct staff interviews, to gather qualitative and quantitative data;

- Task 4 – Analyze quantitative data from CCRTA operating records;

- Task 5 – Identify and analyze financial data and impacts; and

- Task 6 – Write final evaluation report.

It is recommended that the evaluation contract begin as soon as possible and no later than early May 2000, so that revisions to customer survey efforts can be coordinated with CCRTA in time for conducting a fixed-route customer survey in August 2000. Early commencement of the evaluation contract will also help ensure that appropriate data are being archived. It is further recommended that the analysis of both quantitative and qualitative data continue through at least December 2000. This will provide time for system operations to stabilize and for the impacts of the APTS system to become more apparent. It will also provide both a peak (summer) and off-peak (fall/early winter) season to compare Phase 2 "post-implementation" with "pre-implementation" data.

5.1 Initial Coordination

Initial coordination will consist of two primary subtasks:

- Meet with the Volpe Center, the Cape Cod APTS project manager, and CCRTA staff to discuss the current status of the project and finalize the timeline and work steps; and

- Develop a Memorandum of Agreement with CCRTA stating the ways in which CCRTA will assist with the evaluation effort, such as archiving and providing data, participating in interviews, etc.

These subtasks will be conducted in May and June 2000, or immediately after the start of the evaluation contract.

5.2 Customer Surveys

This task will consist of the following subtasks:

- Review past customer surveys conducted by CCRTA and develop recommended changes or additions relevant to the APTS project (May – June 2000);

- Work with CCRTA and their survey contractor to incorporate these changes or additions (July 2000);

- Conduct the customer surveys (August – October 2000, to be performed by CCRTA and their survey contractor); and

- Analyze survey results (September – December 2000).

The three customer surveys conducted by CCRTA during 1998 and 1999 can provide "baseline" or pre-implementation data. Since the last survey was conducted in August 1998, it is recommended that the next fixed-route survey be conducted in August 2000, for seasonal consistency. The previous paratransit survey and general resident survey were conducted in May 1998 and May 1999, respectively. It is recommended that similar surveys be conducted in October 2000. This schedule will provide responses from the off-season, similar to the May surveys, but will also be relatively soon after completion of Phase 2, to be consistent with the other evaluation efforts.

The sampling methodology and design of the revised surveys should remain as consistent as possible so that results between the previous round and this round are comparable. In some cases, it may be necessary to clarify questions or add additional questions relevant to the APTS evaluation. Particular attention should be paid to questions that relate to:

- Customer satisfaction with travel time, reliability, and scheduling requirements;

- Customer satisfaction with the provision of information regarding transit services, as well as media channels used (e.g., Internet); and

- Transportation alternatives, including automobile availability.

Questions that might assist in providing a baseline for evaluation of Phase 3 activities, including the Smart Card and expanded customer information systems, should also be developed. Another round of customer surveys should be planned for 2001 or 2002, once Phase 3 activities have been implemented, and on a seasonal time scale consistent with the surveys that will follow Phase 2 implementation.

It is anticipated that basic tabulations of survey results will be available from the survey contractor. The survey results will also be reviewed to determine whether any additional cross-tabulations or analysis are desired to assess APTS impacts.

5.3 Staff Interviews

Interviews with transit agency staff will be a key component of the evaluation. First, these interviews will provide qualitative information on the various benefits and impacts of the system. This will help characterize the full range and nature of the impacts of the APTS. Staff interviews will also provide quantitative estimates of variables for which other data sources are not available (e.g., changes in incident response time). In some instances, these data may be considered sufficiently reliable to make a quantitative statement about system benefits (e.g., overall delay savings from improved incident response). For other types of data, staff responses may be sufficient only to identify the order of magnitude or relative importance of an impact. This information will help to identify areas in which more detailed collection or analysis of quantitative data may be worthwhile.

The primary interview tasks will include:

- Develop survey questionnaires (May – June 2000);

- Determine personnel to be interviewed (June 2000);

- Set up and conduct round 1 interviews (July – August 2000);

- Produce interim memo documenting round 1 results (September - October 2000);

- Set up and conduct round 2 interviews (January 2001); and

- Document round 2 results in evaluation report (February 2001).

It is recommended that two rounds of interviews be conducted, to gauge any continued changes in operating procedures or impacts over time. The first round should be conducted within two to three months after Phase 2 implementation is complete in May 2000, after staff have had time to learn and adapt to the new technology, but soon enough that both the old and new technologies and procedures are fresh in peoples' minds. The second round should be conducted at least six months (and possibly up to one year) after the first round, to re-assess impacts once the new operational procedures have stabilized and staff are fully comfortable with the new technology.

The choice of staff to interview will be determined in consultation with CCRTA administrative staff. While much of information will be obtained from administrative staff, it will also be desirable to interview a sample of dispatchers, drivers, and possibly maintenance staff. A sufficient sample of each group should be selected to gain a cross-section of opinions and experiences.

5.4 CCRTA System Operating Records

This task involves the review of quantitative data available on CCRTA operations. It includes the following subtasks:

- Coordinate with CCRTA to ensure that available operating data are being archived (May 2000);

- Obtain and review existing databases (e.g., ridership, call tracking, AVL), as well as the MDT data that will exist once Phase 2 is deployed, to determine their specific format, contents, potential uses, and the level of effort that will be required to analyze the data (May – June 2000);

- Develop a plan for any further data processing that may be required (e.g., geocoding of addresses from a sample of trips), as well as statistical analyses and tests that will be conducted on the data. This should be developed in part based on staff interviews indicating what types of benefits are being observed or expected from the APTS system (June – September 2000);

- Prepare and analyze data (September – December 2000).

The appropriate period of analysis will vary depending upon the type of data. Time-series analysis should be conducted on the following data, including periods both before and after deployment of Phase 2:

- Ridership and operating data, including passenger-trips, passenger-miles, passenger-trips per vehicle-hour, etc., for both paratransit and fixed-route systems. This should be analyzed for a three- to five-year period prior to implementation of Phase 2, and for as long a period as possible after Phase 2 deployment. At a minimum, one complete tourist season (Summer 2000) should be analyzed and compared with previous summer seasons. Preferably, observations will continue into the "off-season" and compared with previous periods.

- Data from the paratransit client database including number of clients registered, categorized by automobile ownership, income level, and/or mobility limitation. This should be analyzed on a time scale similar to the ridership and operating data.

- Call tracking system records to determine changes in number of calls handled, average duration of call, etc. This should be evaluated for up to a two-year period prior to Phase 2 deployment as well as up to a one-year period after Phase 2 deployment, although a shorter analysis period should be sufficient. Sampling of daily records during comparable seasons may be considered.

- The potential for analyzing an already geocoded one-week sample of AVL data from Phase 1 should be reviewed. This may provide a "baseline" for comparing vehicle activity to the data gathered by the MDT in Phase 2. The potential benefit of analyzing additional samples should also be considered.

In addition, one-time analysis of the following data will be required:

- Incident records, to estimate total annual incidents, including accidents, by type; and

- Operating statistics required to estimate other benefits and impacts; for example, average vehicle occupancy to determine the benefits of reduced delay.

5.5 Financial Data

This task will involve a review of data on the various costs of the Cape Cod APTS system. It is anticipated that CCRTA will be able to provide data on these costs from its financial records. Primary subtasks will include:

- Collect data from CCRTA on capital costs, known monetary operating and maintenance costs, and labor costs of specific staff positions (June – August 2000);

- Collect data from CCRTA on changes in data transmission costs, equipment, and other outside labor related to APTS components (December 2000 – January 2001);

- Annualize the capital costs, based on assumptions regarding equipment lifecycles and interest rate, and summarize total annual capital and operating costs (January – February 2001).

While final capital costs should be available after Phase 2 deployment is complete, it is recommended that ongoing operating costs be assessed later, after changes in operating procedures have stabilized and longer-term operating cost changes have become apparent. The operating cost data should be reviewed over a period of time before and after deployment and should be reviewed for any seasonal changes (e.g., higher loads during the summer), so that comparable "before" and "after" observations can be established.

5.6 Evaluation Report

Writing the evaluation report will be conducted in two primary stages:

- A draft report, to be delivered to Volpe in February 2001; and

- A final report, to be completed by April 2001.

The evaluation report will summarize the methodologies and key findings of the various evaluation tasks described above. To the extent possible, it will synthesize the findings to describe the overall benefits and costs of the APTS project as a whole and its individual components. The report will also discuss any particular local or project-specific factors, such as institutional and environmental factors, that may have significantly affected the various benefits and costs of the project. This assessment will help other agencies determine the transferability and relevance of the evaluation results to their situation.

Finally, the evaluation report will identify any areas in which continued changes in costs and benefits are expected, both as a result of long-term impacts of the Phase 1 and 2 technologies, and as a result of Phase 3 technologies that may be implemented in the future.

6.0 Evaluation Management Plan

6.1 Organization and Responsibilities of the Evaluation Project Team

This evaluation is sponsored by the U.S. DOT ITS Joint Program Office. ITS JPO has contracted with the Volpe National Transportation Systems Center to coordinate the evaluation and perform cross-cutting studies. The Volpe Center will contract with an independent consultant to conduct the evaluation of the Cape Cod APTS project. This independent evaluation will determine how well the Cape Cod APTS project fulfills the objectives of both the CCRTA and the APTS program. As indicated by federal requirements, the CCRTA will also carry out its own local evaluation to determine how this project meets local objectives. Relevant findings from the local evaluation will be incorporated into the nationally-sponsored evaluation report to provide a broader picture of the impacts of the project.

6.2 Timeline and Milestones

Table 6.1 shows a project timeline, based on the various tasks described in Section 5. The evaluation products and milestones will include:

- Agreement between the evaluator, CCRTA, and survey contractor on revised customer survey design and timeline (May or June 2000);

- A Memorandum of Understanding between the evaluator and CCRTA, indicating agreement on the ways in which CCRTA will support the evaluation activities (June 2000);

- Technical memorandum #1: Results of round 1 staff interviews (mid-October 2000);

- Technical memorandum #2: Detailed analysis plan for quantitative data (mid-October 2000);

- Draft evaluation report (February 2001); and

- Final evaluation report (April 2001).

Table 6.1 Cape Cod APTS Evaluation Timeline

Task	Description	2000 May	June	July	August	Sept.	Oct.	Nov.	Dec.	2001 Jan.	Feb.	March	April
1	**Initial Coordination**												
	Kick-Off Meeting	█											
	Memorandum of Agreement	█											
2	**Customer Surveys**												
	Develop, incorporate changes		█	█									
	Conduct surveys (CCRTA)				█	█	█						
	Analyze results							█					
3	**Staff Interviews**												
	Develop questionnaires		█	█									
	Round 1 interviews				█								
	Interim memo on Round 1 results					█	█						
	Round 2 interviews									█			
4	**Operating Data**												
	Obtain and review databases		█	█									
	Develop analysis plan					█							
	Process and analyze data						█	█					
5	**Financial Data**												
	Collect capital cost data		█										
	Collect operating cost data								█				
	Analyze cost data									█	█		
6	**Evaluation Report**												
	Develop draft report									█	█		
	Develop final report											█	█

6.3 Budget

Table 6.2 outlines the estimated staff time required by the consultant to conduct the evaluation after this evaluation plan has been approved. In summary, the evaluation will require approximately 780 hours of consultant staff time. The approximate cost associated with this level of effort will be $80,000. The cost and level of effort noted here do not include the development and completion of this evaluation plan document.

Table 6.2 Level of Effort (Person-Hours)

Task	Description	Senior	Middle	Junior	Admin.	Total
1.	Initial Coordination	8	32			40
2.	Customer Surveys	4	32			36
3.	Staff Interviews	4	160			164
4.	Operating Data	12	160	100	40	312
5.	Financial Data	4	88			92
6.	Evaluation Report	8	88		40	136
	Total Hours	**40**	**560**	**100**	**80**	**780**